ECONOMIC
IMPERIALISM

ECONOMIC IMPERIALISM

By
LEONARD WOOLF

NEW YORK

Howard Fertig

1970

First published in 1920

HOWARD FERTIG, INC. EDITION 1970
Published by arrangement with the author.

Library of Congress Catalog Card Number: 68-9627

PRINTED IN THE UNITED STATES OF AMERICA
BY NOBLE OFFSET PRINTERS, INC.

CONTENTS

CHAPTER I

INTRODUCTORY

THE subject of this book is the relation of European States to the undeveloped countries of Asia and Africa. Individually we are to-day spectators of and participants in a world movement which is having the most profound effects upon our lives and upon the lives of the inhabitants of Asia and Africa. Great world movements like that of Christianity, feudalism, the war of 1914, and the phenomena which will be examined in these pages, appear to the ordinary man, particularly when he is a contemporary, to be completely out of his control. They seem to come upon him and upon the world with the inevitability of some great natural force, the earthquake, the monsoon, or the change from winter to summer, and from summer back again to winter. This fatalistic view of history, though it is comforting to many people and to historians, is a delusion. Man has achieved so large a victory over natural forces and his distant relations of the animal world, that his history is now but little influenced by them. The history of man has, in the last 2500 years been mainly determined by man, by his beliefs and by his desires. If certain men had not begun to believe and desire certain things, there would have been no Christians and no Christianity, and if certain other men had not believed and desired certain other things, there would have been no persecution of the early Christians; and the failure of Christianity to produce a Christian world has resulted from a victory of the desires and beliefs of the one over those of the other. It was not God nor kings who for centuries bound Europe in the chains of the feudal system : feudalism was produced by what went on in the minds of dozens of lords and thousands of serfs, the tremendous effect of which is obscured by the fantastic romance which we call history. It was not the Kaiser or any other " war criminal " who caused the Great War, but the millions of men and women who read the German, English, and French papers, believed what those papers told them to believe and desired what those papers told them to desire.

The relation between Europeans and non-Europeans, between European civilisation and

non-European civilisations, was so profoundly modified during the nineteenth century that the changes
have now constituted a world movement whose
effects are as deep and as wide and as drastic as
those of Christianity or feudalism. A bare com-
parison of the world of 1800 with the world of
1900 will reveal immediately the essential nature of
these tremendous changes. In 1800 certain
portions of the world outside Europe had suffered
varying degrees of Europeanisation, but little
territory and few peoples had been subjected to
the control and the forcible Europeanisation of
European States. To-day practically the whole of
the world which has not been Europeanised has
been subjected openly or covertly to European
control. Let us examine a little more closely the
changes of this century. A hundred years ago the
continent of America had been partially Europeanised through the early Portuguese and
Spanish conquests and the later French and
Anglo-Saxon invasions. The European had
scarcely penetrated into Africa ; the European
State had no foothold in the vast territories of
Asia, although a British commercial company
had established itself in some parts of India, and
Holland, Portugal, and France still boasted some

small possessions ; in the Pacific and the great Australian continent there was no effective penetration of or control by Europeans. To-day the whole of North America has been completely and South America mainly Europeanised ; every square foot of Africa, with the doubtful exception of Abyssinia and Liberia has been partitioned by and subjected to the direct control of European States ; in Asia there is only one people, the Japanese, which can be said to be completely independent of European control, and immense areas have been partitioned among or conquered by European States ; all the islands of the Pacific are either possessions or colonies of European States.

Here then is a world movement which consists of a Europeanisation of the world. But there are two processes operating in this movement. The first is what I have called in the previous paragraph " Europeanisation." It is an old phenomenon in human history. Tribes, and races, and peoples have always ebbed and flowed over the earth's surface, and in the colonisation of America, South Africa, and Australia, we have modern examples of such tides in the history of the human race. Such colonisation may begin with slaughter and conquest, but it at least ends in the creation of a new civilisation, rooted in the soil, controlling its own affairs in its own way. In America, South Africa (to some extent), and the Pacific, the European conqueror or colonist has either fused with the native population or has himself multiplied to form new and independent communities with their own civilisation and their own government. But in Asia and in Africa a different process has taken place, and it is this which I propose to examine in these pages. In Africa, except in a small area in the south, there has been no colonisation, no fusion of races, no growth of a new population or civilisation. The land and peoples have simply been conquered and subjected to the direct and autocratic rule of European States In Asia, as I shall show, the movement has taken two different forms : in India and in parts of China and territory bordering upon China the power of the European State has been used directly, as in Africa, to acquire and to subject the populations to European rule ; but in China itself, in Persia, and in Turkey, the power of the European State has been applied indirectly, not to acquire territory and complete administrative control of the population, but in order to further the economic interests of the inhabitants of the European State.

It is this two-fold process, operating in Africa and Asia, which I shall examine and discuss in the following pages. It will be necessary to deal with its two forms separately, but here it will be useful to go a little more deeply into its general characteristics. The phenomenon which we shall study is really the relations of Europeans to non-Europeans in Africa and Asia as they have crystallised in the policy of European States towards the peoples and Governments of the two Continents. That policy has resulted, as we have seen, in the subjection of the whole of Africa and almost the whole of Asia to the direct or indirect control of European States. The really important question for us is what have been the motives, objects, and results of this policy; what were the motives with which Europeans and their States have proceeded to subject these distant lands and peoples to their control; what have been the objects and the results of the control when once established. Now the motives of men and nations and States are not simple, and it would be absurdly false to pretend to find a single and simple cause for the complex phenomenon of the partition of Africa, the conquest of India, or the exploitation of China. But while large historical events and movements are moulded by all kinds of different causes, it is also true that often one particular cause stands out pre-eminent as the real motive power behind the changes. This is certainly true of the European policy in Africa and Asia during the last fifty years. The policy has resulted in the carving up of the two continents among a few European Great Powers into empires or imperial possessions and spheres of influence or of exploitation. This would not have happened, had not Europeans had certain beliefs and desires. These beliefs and desires which have produced European imperialism in Africa and Asia can be analysed into four different kinds, moral, sentimental, military and economic ; and we must briefly examine what part each kind played in forming the imperialist policy of European States.

The conception of the moral nature and duty of imperialism, the idea that the rule of Asiatics and Africans and the acquisition of their territory by Europeans is morally justifiable and necessary, often occur in the speeches and the writings of imperialists. The doctrine has been summed up in a phrase, " the white man's burden." According to this historical and political vision, the white man is superior to other races, in heart and brain, above all in his political and social institutions, his morality, and his religion ; he is in fact one more of God's Chosen Peoples. As in Canaan, 2,000 years ago, so in Africa and Asia to-day, the first duty of the Chosen People is to subjugate the rest of the world as a preliminary to conferring on it the blessings of the superior civilisation. And if the inferior races obstinately refuse to acknowledge their position and to accept the blessings, they must, unfortunately, be conquered and killed until they accept the law of God and of the conquerors.. There is no doubt that these moral ideas have to some extent entered into the doctrine and policy of imperialism ; but it is important to be clear as to the exact way in which they entered. In the nineteenth century moral ideas have never been the motive or motive power in any imperialist adventure. No European State ever conquered or acquired control over any African or Asiatic territory or people in order to confer upon that people the blessings of European rule. It is impossible to point to a single instance in which even the alleged motive at the time was the good of the conquered or of the acquired. When territory has been acquired, the arguments for the adventure have always been, before the acquisition, either

military, economic, or sentimental (prestige).
The European State has always had either (1) to
punish someone for not being European and
civilised (military punitive expeditions), or (2)
to protect someone already conquered and acquired
from the bad example of uncivilised and unconquered neighbours (military punitive expeditions),
or (3) to avenge an insult to the flag (sentimental-
prestige), or (4) to protect or to further the economic
interests of the European subjects of the State.
These facts were, indeed, so obvious that towards
the end of the last century imperialists ceased to
argue that Empires had been or should be acquired
for the good of the subject peoples.   The moral
argument and ideas, however, still continued to
form a halo round imperialism.   If it was no longer
argued that Europe conquered or subjected Africa
and Asia for the good of Africans and Asiatics,
or to spread among them the blessings of civilisation, Christianity, law, and order, the good of
the subject peoples was and still is frequently used
as an argument against withdrawing from a conquest once it has been made, or abandoning
control once it has been acquired.   Thus no one
now pretends that France went into Tunis, or
Britain into Egypt or Uganda, for altruistic

motives ; on the other hand, the good of the
Egyptians and Tunisians has so far again and
again prevented the British and French from ful-
filling their promises to evacuate Egypt and Tunis ;
and when once Captain Lugard had acquired
Uganda for a British joint-stock company, the
chief and most telling argument against abandonment was the irreparable damage which evacuation
would cause to the people of Uganda, to Christianity, and to British trade.   Thus, to sum up,
the connection between imperialism and moral
ideas appears to be this : Europeans have acquired
their Empires for selfish motives ; they, or many
of them, believe that they retain and maintain their
empires for altruistic motives.   The white man's
burden becomes a duty only after, in a fit of absence
of mind or in order to fill his pockets, he has placed
it upon his own shoulders.

Sentiment and sentimentality have always played
some part in imperialism.   It gives full play to the
romance which attaches to the adventure of conquest and war, provided that they are carried on at
a distance sufficiently far to spare us any actual
experience of them.   In fact, the first stage in the
acquisition of territory by modern empires is
often a private adventure by some romantic

adventurer or sentimental soldier who cannot find*
what he seeks among the industrialised cities of
Europe, but can satisfy his desires for wandering,
killing, and conquering among the fortunate and
less civilised inhabitants of Asia and Africa. But
it would be a mistake to consider that the ideas of
sentimental adventurers were ever a determining
cause of the imperialist expansion of European
States during the last hundred years. The passion
for adventure in some colonial governor or soldier
may have, particularly in India, furnished a
convenient excuse and starting point for a policy
of expansion, but no State or statesman has ever
professed a policy or acknowledged a duty of
providing in an African and Asiatic Empire a field
for the activities of their more restless and romantic subjects. More influence has been exercised
upon imperial policy by another and more important sentimental belief. In France, Britain,
Germany, and Italy the speeches of responsible and
irresponsible statesmen and the writings of historians and publicists show a very widely and
firmly held belief that the acquisition and retention
of imperial possessions and dependencies outside
Europe reflects great glory on the European State.

* I am speaking of the period before 1914.

According to this philosophy the prestige of a State is very seriously affected by whether it has or has not conquered savages. In fact the glory of a European nation is not only increased by the acquisition of territory outside Europe ; it appears to be also diminished by the mere fact of such acquisition by some other nation. We have the authority of a French Prime Minister for the doctrine that the seizure of Cyprus by Britain was a blow at the prestige of France, and that the glory of France could only recover its brightness through the French seizure of some other territory either in Tonkin or Tunis, or preferably in both. The acquisition of South-West Africa and other colonies by Germany is frequently represented by British historians and politicians as striking at, not only Britain's commercial and strategic interests, but also at her prestige. It may be of interest to note that this strange phenomenon in the world and psychology of nations has its counterpart in the world and psychology of classes. The acquisition of white lace-curtains and an aspidistra, or in another class of a motor car or a footman, confers social prestige ; but everyone must have observed the further fact that the acquisition of one of these possessions by an individual A, is regarded as an affront to the prestige of an individual B, who does not possess one, when A and B are of the same class. But although the belief that imperial possessions add to the dignity and glory of the State has certainly influenced the policy of the Great Powers, this belief has done very little to set that policy in motion. It is significant that no imperialist statesman has ever ventured, when setting out on some imperialist adventure, to state publicly that he was proposing to acquire territory or a sphere of influence in order to add to the prestige of his country, while in similar circumstances the public statement has often been made that the policy is rendered necessary in order to protect or to further the economic interests of his country. The modern State has frequently destroyed the independence of African or Asiatic peoples on the pretext that their uncivilised rulers or Government have insulted the honour of the European State (*e.g.* France conquered Algeria because its ruler flicked the French Consul in the face with a fly-whisk), but the belief that conquest is legitimate merely because it is glorious is no longer accepted by common people and cannot be said to have played any large part in the Europeanisation of Africa and Asia during the last century. The truth appears to be that, as causes in the complex phenomenon of imperialist policy, sentimental beliefs hold the some position as moral. The idea that empire is glory is used as an argument or motive not for acquiring empire but for retaining it, when acquired. What usually happens is that imperialist adventures are started and put through secretly by a few soldiers, capitalists, and statesmen, and the ordinary Briton, Frenchman, or German, wakes up one morning to discover that he has acquired or is in process of acquiring territory or a sphere of influence outside Europe.* There has always been a small party in these three countries opposed to such acquisitions, and the " anti-imperialists," finding themselves faced with the accomplished fact, can only face it by demanding evacuation or abandonment. It is at this moment that the imperialists find the sentimental and moral arguments and beliefs most useful. If the empire is glorious, there is an obvious relation between imperialism and patriotism, and it becomes unpatriotic to say a word against either imperialism or the empire, or to urge the abandonment of any

* This is true of the British acquisition of East Africa, Nigeria, and the greater part of our Asiatic Empire, the German acquisition of all her colonial Empire, and the French acquisition of Algeria, Tunis, Morocco, etc.

imperial acquisition. And the larger the empire, the more glorious it is, and the more unpatriotic to diminish a ray of its glory or an inch of its territory. Thus patriotism and morality combine not to cause imperialism, but to suppress discussion of or opposition to empire.

The position of military or strategic beliefs and desires as a cause of European expansion outside Europe is clear, but is frequently misunderstood. In certain limited areas like the Mediterranean, strategic reasons have had some effect on the creation of imperialist policy in Mediterranean States, *e.g.*, France and Italy. The acquisition of Algeria, Tunis, and Morocco by France, and of Tripoli by Italy, has been defended on the grounds of military necessity. The argument here has been " Unless we seize this territory, the other country may seize it and use it as a base for military operations against us." But the argument applies to, and has only rarely been applied to, a very limited stretch of African territory, facing the coasts of Italy and France. The rest of Asia and Africa lies too far distant from Europe for its possession to affect the strategic safety of any European territory or State. In fact no imperialist has ever pretended that the acquisition of Empire on the East

or West Coast of Africa or in Asia was necessary for
the military or naval safety of the mother country.
But, as soon as an imperial acquisition is made,
the whole position changes. The Imperial State
now has to afford military protection not only to its
home territory but to its colonial possessions. It
becomes at once possible to argue that more territory must be acquired in order to ensure the
military protection of territory already acquired.
Thus Britain holds Egypt not because Egypt
protects Britain strategically, but because, if she
did not hold Egypt, she could not hold India.
Military reasons are, therefore, not to any great
extent a cause of imperialism, but they are a reason
for making an empire large, and a large empire
larger.

It will be seen that these three kinds of beliefs,
moral, sentimental, strategic, all affect men's
ideas and ideals of empire, and therefore they have
influenced the policy of imperialism. But they are
not fundamental. They would not of themselves,
either collectively or singly, have been sufficient
to set in motion or to maintain in motion the
expansion of Europe and the subjection of Africa
and Asia which we are studying in these pages.
The truth of this statement can be demonstrated.

Suppose that the European had only had these moral, sentimental, and strategic ideas with regard to territory and people outside Europe. Then it is certain that the whole history of the last half century would have been completely different ; there would have been no world movement of expansion and no wholesale subjection of two continents. A fringe of the northern coast of Africa would probably have been divided between France and Italy ; the British Empire might have retained Cape Colony, and have completed the conquest of India ; adventurous and sentimental soldiers and sailors would probably have seen to it that the States which they served seized from time to time a few small and ill-defined possessions on African coasts or on the mouths of Asiatic rivers ; missionaries would have borne the main weight of the white man's burden by carrying the gospel of Christ and European civilisation to black, brown, and yellow heathens and by finding saintly and heroic tombs in far-off lands, or even, occasionally, in their inhabitants. But most Africans and Asiatics would now be living in possession and full control of their own countries, unconquered by and not subjected to Europeans, enjoying under their native institutions and economic and governmental systems that incompetence and disorder which the European boasts that he has eradicated.

If we turn now to economic beliefs, desires, and causes, we find an entirely different state of affairs. At every step in the imperialist expansion of Europe, the impulse of economic causes is evident. And here it is necessary to point out that there are two clearly defined periods in the history of economic imperialism. Up to about forty or fifty years ago the new economic and industrial system in Europe, and the economic ideals of its inhabitants, caused a certain amount of penetration (and sometimes of subjection) of Asia and Africa by Europeans. But this movement was spasmodic, largely unconscious, and it rarely influenced the policy of European States. The relations between the three continents were almost entirely economic, but they consisted of private commercial undertakings and adventures by which foreign markets were found for the products of European industry and these were exchanged for the products and raw materials of Asia, and to a less extent of Africa. The undertakings were in every sense private, and sprang from the desire and principle which is the bedrock of European civilisation, to sell in the dearest and to buy in the cheapest market. They sometimes led to the acquisition of large areas of territory by commercial companies or to serious difficulties between the traders and native governments ; and these events again occasionally led to intervention of European governments. But European States and governments did not acknowledge, and were not expected to acknowledge, any responsibility for pushing or for protecting the economic interests of their European subjects outside Europe, and the world had not yet heard of the idea, which is now the first principle of policy, that the organised power of the State should be consciously and ruthlessly applied to the furthering of those interests.

In the last twenty or thirty years of the century all this was altered. A profound change came over the political and economic outlook of Europe, and suddenly produced the outbreak of economic imperialism as we know it. The outbreak was as sudden as the outburst of leaves and buds in spring, but, just as the spectacular budding and flowering of spring under a few hours of warm sunshine are really caused by slow and unseen changes which have been going on all through the winter in plant and tree, so too the gradual change which has been working in

European society and the European's ideas and ideals ever since the industrial revolution caused a condition of the world in which the casual combination of a few events produced a fundamental change in the world's government and a catastrophic re-arrangement of human society.

The industrial revolution had produced an industrialised society. The population of Europe was increasing enormously, and great masses of it were being concentrated in towns and industrial centres. Two results sprang from this. In order to feed and employ the ever growing millions engaged in European industry, the food products and raw materials of the rest of the world had to be made available for Europeans. Secondly, since industry was carried on under the capitalist system, it was axiomatic that the exchange of the food products and raw materials of extra-European territory for the manufactured products of European industry should result in the maximum of profit to the small class who provided the capital for and controlled the operations of industry. In those conditions economic interests, and the complex of beliefs and desires which gathered round them, became more and more insistent, and the springs of human action were no longer to be found in religious, moral, or caste beliefs, but in the principle of profit-making, of buying in the cheapest and selling in the dearest market. Every instrument was seized upon which could possibly be used to further the economic interests of the nation, class, or individual, and among such instruments obviously one of the most powerful was the organised power of the modern State. Politics became another name for economics and the relation of the State to the economic interests of citizens, according to this new religion or philosophy, is shown by Chamberlain's belief, universally accepted and acted upon, that " commerce is the greatest of all political interests."

About 1870 Europe had just become ripe for economic imperialism. It already believed that economic were the greatest of all interests and it was slowly acquiring the belief that the power of each state should be used in the world outside the State to promote the interests of its own citizens and against the interests of citizens of other States. Two events combined to bring about the sudden flowering and fruiting of these beliefs and desires in the subjection of Asia and Africa to the economic interests of Europe. Between 1870 and 1880 the interior of Africa and its apparently inexhaustible riches were finally opened to the world by the well-advertised explorations and discoveries of Stanley. At the same moment there was beginning the change from the policy of Free Trade to the policy of protectionism. It was the beliefs and desires contained in this policy of protectionism, which, when applied to the problem of the newly opened lands of Africa, and then by analogy to Asia, produced economic imperialism. For the theory and practice of protectionism which established themselves between 1870 and 1880, implied that the organisation of the State should be used as a weapon against the industrial and commercial interests of the citizens of other States. A ring fence of tariffs and administrative regulations was to be drawn round the territory under the control of the State in order to reserve within it for its own citizens the markets and the stores of raw materials. These new conceptions, or rather this return to the old conceptions of mercantilism, roused in the capitalist, industrial, and commercial circles of every European nation mingled emotions of cupidity and fear, and since those circles were beginning to exercise great influence upon the policy of the Great Powers, the emotions and the beliefs behind them were clearly reflected in

European policy between 1870 and 1914. The fear was the fear of being shut out from the profitable markets of Europe with its growing population, and of being shut out from the stores of raw materials and food supplies essential for large scale industrial production in towns ; the cupidity lay in the desire for profit resulting from success in shutting out your foreign rivals.

The policy of protectionism began on the continent of Europe and in the United States of North America, but it was soon seen that its implications stretched out to embrace Asia and Africa. Men turned, again with fear and cupidity, to the markets composed of the potential demands of millions of Asiatics and Africans and to the vast stores of raw materials lying in the rich lands of those two continents. No one knew when the shutter of a protectionist tariff might not descend and shut him off from some European market or from some essential raw material for his industry, and it was natural that the captains of trade and industry should seek to insure themselves against such European disasters by making their position secure in the markets, the mines, and the forests of Asia and Africa. But the nemesis of economic cupidity and fear cannot be confined to one of the world's continents. If industry and trade were to be converted into a struggle and war between organised national States in Europe, what was to prevent it becoming a war too outside Europe ? If the French capitalist and manufacturer, using the power and organisation of his State, shut the British out of France, would he not also do the same in Algeria ? And what France had done in Algeria, in northern Africa, she or some other State might proceed to do again in the Eldorado which Stanley was rumoured to have discovered in central Africa, or in the vast, rich, thickly populated countries of Asia. Why, it was already whispered that King Leopold of Belgium, under the pretence of science and philanthropy, was using Stanley and his explorations to win the new Eldorado for himself and Belgium.

So men began to argue about the year 1880. The effect upon foreign policy was instantaneous. The " Great Powers," France, Germany, and Britain fell upon Africa and Asia, seizing territory wherever they could lay hands on it. In the ten years 1880-1890, five million square miles of African territory, containing a population of over sixty millions, were seized by and subjected to European States. In Asia during the same ten years Britain annexed Burma and subjected to her control the Malay peninsula and Baluchistan ; while France took the first steps towards subjecting or breaking up China by seizing Annam and Tonking. At the same time there took place a scramble for the islands of the Pacific between the three Great Powers.

The next two chapters will show in some detail the immense part which economic causes played in this outburst of imperialist activities. Here two points may be noticed. First, over and over again the immediate impulse towards the European State's intervention in Asia and Africa, its annexations, protectorates, or penetration, came from financiers or capitalist joint-stock companies. In German East Africa, British East Africa, Nyasaland, South Africa, German West Africa, Nigeria, the Congo, British North Borneo, chartered or unchartered companies paved the way to empire by extracting treaties from native chiefs and rulers purporting to hand over the sovereignty in these vast territories to the joint-stock companies. Elsewhere in Cameroon and Togoland, Italian Somaliland, and the French Congo, financiers, traders, and companies laid the foundations and supplied the impetus of the subsequent annexation. Thus the economic beliefs and desires can be seen to have been completely different in their effects from the sentimental, moral, and military causes which we examined above : they supplied the original motive power which set in motion the power of the State.

But that is not all. The policies of States emanate from Governments, and Governments are composed of statesmen and politicians. If we turn to the speeches of the statesmen who were responsible for this imperialist policy during 1880 to 1914, we can learn the reasons for that policy which they gave in defending it and explaining it to the peoples of France, Britain, and Germany. In France the protagonists in that policy were Jules Ferry, Saint-Hilaire, and Etienne. All three agree in affirming that the main motives of their policy were economic. It was essential, they said, that France should acquire an empire in Asia and Africa in order to provide outlets for her industries and capital (débouchés pour nos industries, nos exportations, nos capitaux) and in order to ensure her food supplies and her supplies of raw material. In Britain the spokesmen of the new imperialism were

Joseph Chamberlain and Lord Rosebery. Mr. Chamberlain declared that the care of his Government was that " new markets shall be created, and that old markets shall be effectually developed," and he explained that there was therefore " a necessity, as well as a duty, for us to uphold the dominion and empire which we now possess," and a " necessity for using every legitimate opportunity to extend our influence and control in that African continent which is now being opened up to civilisation and to commerce." Lord Rosebery expressed the same view in a sentence when he described the subjection of territory outside Europe to the British State as a necessary process by which the British were " pegging out claims for posterity." In Germany the first steps towards a colonial empire were taken by Bismarck, though he was no imperialist. He took those steps under pressure from commercial and industrial circles, and he made it perfectly clear that his action was governed by economic reasons : he wanted, he said, outside Europe " not provinces, but commercial enterprises."

The motive power, therefore, behind modern imperialism is economic ; it springs from economic beliefs and desires. There are other ingredients in the ferment which has caused the Europeanisation of Africa and Asia, but if they had all been absent and the economic causes and motives had remained, the same effects would have resulted. That is why we are justified in calling this process economic imperialism.

NOTE.

The reader will find the subject of this chapter much more fully developed in my book *Empire and Commerce in Africa*.

CHAPTER II

ECONOMIC IMPERIALISM IN AFRICA

THE area of Africa is about 11,500,000 square
miles, and its population about 170 millions. In
1880 less than 1,000,000 square miles with a
population of under ten millions were in the
hands of European States. By 1890, 6,000,000
square miles had been annexed by Britain,
Germany, France, Belgium, and Portugal. By
1914 the whole continent, with the exception of
Abyssinia (350,000 square miles and eight millions
population) and Liberia (area 40,000 square miles,
population two millions), had been subjected to
the control and government of European States.
The following figures show what shares the
various States took in this partition :

		Area	Population.
France	..	4,200,000	25,000,000
Britain	..	3,300,000	35,000,000
Germany	..	1,100,000	12,000,000
Belgium	..	900,000	7,000,000
Portugal	..	800,000	8,000,000
Italy	..	600,000	1,000,000
Spain	..	75,000	200,000

As to the actual process of partition, something must be added to what has already been said in the previous chapter. Two different methods were practised by European States in subjecting Africa. In 1880 a few States, like Britain, France, and Portugal, already had a small foothold in various parts of the continent, *e.g.* France held Algeria and small undefined possessions in Senegal and Gabun ; Britain held Cape Colony and three small colonies on the west coast ; Portugal had old standing claims to an undefined area both on the west and east coasts. When in the 'eighties the policy of economic imperialism began to assert itself, it was natural that these three States should make their possessions jumping off places for further expansion. This they did either by laying claim to enormous and undefined areas of land lying around the original possession and then by attempting to " make their occupation effective," or by finding some pretext for military operations against and conquest of the neighbouring tribes or native rulers. It was by this method that the French added Tunis to Algeria, the Saharan empire to Tunis and Algeria, and eventually rounded off their Mediterranean African empire by annexing Morocco. At the same time by a vast number of military expeditions, often disguised under the name of " scientific expeditions " or " explorations," sent out from her possessions on the north and west coasts into the interior, France succeeded in establishing claims to a vast hinterland behind her scattered possessions. The idea was to join up these various hinterlands until they formed one solid block of empire debouching on the West coast in the Congo, Nigeria, Dahomey, the Ivory Coast, and Senegal, on the Mediterranean in Morocco, Algeria, and Tunis, and on the east coast in Somaliland. This policy, consciously and deliberately pursued by French Governments under the guidance of French " colonial circles," was almost completely successful. It met with only two checks or failures, both at the hands of Britain. It failed in its attempt to establish French dominion over the territory, economically most important, at the mouth of the Niger River, and after a bitter quarrel between the two countries Nigeria was seized by Britain. French imperialists also failed in their attempt to obtain possession of the Nile Valley, and so to join up their possessions on the west coast with French Somaliland, and here again after a bitter struggle between France and Britain which ended with the victory and defeat

Fashoda again

at Fashoda, French imperialism had to give way
to British.

French Imperialism in Africa has differed somewhat from that of the other European States (except
Italy) by having used almost exclusively as its
instrument of expansion this weapon of military
expeditions and conquest. It would be impossible
for anyone to say of the French African empire,
what has been falsely said of the British, that it
was won in a fit of absence of mind. On the con-
trary it was, to quote the words of a French
historian, " the result of a political plan carefully
studied, applied methodically in the face of great
difficulties, and finally realised with complete
success." This method of expansion according
to a political plan and by means of military conquest was, however, not confined to France.
In Egypt in the north and Cape Colony in the
south Britain used precisely the same political and
military methods for increasing her imperial
dominions. At Fashoda the world saw a strong
British force under Kitchener face to face with a
weak French force under Marchand, and the danger
of the crisis lay in the fact that each had received
the orders of his Government to establish effective
occupation of the Nile Valley.   Again the expansion

of the British Empire northwards from Cape
Colony was accomplished by a series of wars of
conquest, the Zulu war of 1879, the conquest of
Mashonaland 1890, the Matabele War of 1893, and
the Boer War of 1899. All these wars were wars of
conquest planned and pursued with great delibera-
tion. Thus the Zulu war of 1879, which resulted in
the annexation of Zululand in 1887, was due to the
deliberate policy of Sir Bartle Frere, Governor of
the Cape. " A man of clear and far-reaching
aims," says *The Cambridge Modern History*, " he
believed that British sovereignty must sooner or
later be extended over the whole of South Africa
as far north as the Portuguese dominions. He
therefore accepted the annexation of the Transvaal,
made war on the troublesome Transkei Kafirs,
and, while conceding to the Zulus most of the land
in dispute, demanded of Cetewayo the immediate
dissolution of his military policy. The result was
a war which lasted through the first seven months
of 1879." We may remark here a confirmation
of the truth pointed out in our first chapter with
regard to the position of men's beliefs and desires
as historical causes. If States appoint as
Governors of small colonial possessions men who
believe and desire that the sovereignty of the State

must be extended over several million square
miles and millions of people who do not desire to
be conquered or reduced to subjection, the result,
as in South Africa, will inevitably be a series of
wars.

The military nature of this expansion of the
French and British empires must not, however,
obscure the compelling part played in it by
economic motives. The weapon of expansion was
war and conquest, the aims of expansion were
markets, raw materials, and profits. We have
already referred to the policy of Jules Ferry which
caused the first onslaught of French imperialism,
the invasion and conquest of Tunis in 1881. The
subjection of Tunis was a classical example of
economic imperialism. In the 'sixties and
'seventies Tunis, under the government of a
native bey, and nominally under the suzerainty of
Turkey, was penetrated economically by a horde of
French speculators, financiers, concessionaires,
and adventurers. They were successful in ruining
the country. Lending money at usurious rates
to the bey, they got him to make over to them in
return the most valuable economic concessions.
The bey, heavily in the debt of Paris capitalists and
financiers, was compelled to fleece his subjects in

order to pay interest on the loans. The inhabitants were in a constant state of rebellion against this process by which they were reduced to penury in order to feed the Paris money market. The financiers and concessionaires then appealed to the French Government to protect their interests in Tunis against the " chronic disorder " of the Tunisians. The Government of Jules Ferry was not deaf to their appeal. The French Premier sent an army into Tunis to put down the disorders and to protect the interests of French subjects. But everyone in Paris knew that the motives of this military expedition were economic. M. Clemenceau said in the French Chamber that the whole thing was a " coup de Bourse " and, as we have pointed out, Jules Ferry himself, when he defended his policy in the Chamber, did so by arguing that Tunis was necessary for France as " an outlet for our manufactures " and as " a lucrative means of investing capital."

French colonial policy after Ferry owed nearly everything to one man, M. Etienne, who was Under-Secretary of State for the Colonies from 1887 to 1892. It was M. Etienne who invented, or at least carried through, the policy of incessant military and quasi-military expeditions which added millions of square miles of territory to the French African Empire. But the motives of M. Etienne's military imperialism were the same as Ferry's ; they were economic. It is possible to prove this conclusively. In 1894 the struggle between Britain and France for control of the Nile Valley, a struggle which was to end at Fashoda in 1898, entered upon its critical and final stage. M. Etienne came down to the Chamber of Deputies to urge upon the Government of the day a forward policy on the part of France in the face of British hostility. In doing so he explained quite clearly what had been the motives of his own policy of expansion through military and " scientific " expeditions. " We have built up," he said, " and we intend to preserve and develop, a colonial empire in order to assure the future of our country in the new continents, in order to reserve there an outlet for our products (un débouché à nos marchandises) and to find there raw materials for our industries."

Now, if we turn to Britain, we find precisely the same causes acting behind the policy of military expansion in Africa. Mr. Chamberlain defended our " continued occupation of Egypt " in order that " new markets shall be created and that old

markets shall be effectually developed," and it
is significant that three years before Fashoda it was
the London Chamber of Commerce which called
upon the Government of which Mr. Chamberlain
was a distinguished and powerful member, " to
take adequate measures with a view to assuring
control of England over the whole valley of the
Nile from Uganda to Fashoda." Again there is
clear evidence of the overwhelming part played
by economic beliefs and desires in British military
expansion in the south of Africa. In Cape Colony
itself there was always during the 'eighties a
party working for British expansion in the north
by means of wars and military expeditions. Their
motives may be judged from the statement of the
Prime Minister of Cape Colony in 1884 that " very
many people in the colony were for direct imperial
intervention, but most of those had selfish ends to
serve ; they wished for troops that they might
enrich themselves by getting good contracts."
But still more significant are the motives of the
broader and less immediately selfish imperialist
policy in South Africa of which the directing spirit
was Cecil Rhodes. This policy, most persistently
pursued throughout the 'eighties and 'nineties, was
the same as that of Sir Bartle Frere in 1879. It

aimed at bringing under British control, preferably by " negotiations " but, if necessary by war
and conquest, the whole of the north of South
Africa and its native inhabitants. It was an
integral part of this policy to hem in the Transvaal
Republic in order to prevent it acquiring any
additional territory in Bechuanaland on the west,
or any territory on the east, which might give it
access to the sea and to a port. The effect of this
policy upon the peace of South Africa and upon the
relations between Dutch and British there may be
studied in the detailed account of Dr. W. J.
Leyds.* Here we can only briefly draw attention
to the persistence of the economic motive in this
policy. As early as 1884 when the London Con-
vention between the Transvaal and the British was
being negotiated we find Rhodes telegraphing to
the Cape Premier : " Don't part with one inch of
territory to Transvaal." Already in those early
days the question was one of pure economic
imperialism. The territory in question was that of
Bechuanaland, and the immediate problem was to
draw a boundary between the Transvaal and
British territory or sphere. What Rhodes was
anxious about and what the negotiations actually

* *The Transvaal Surrounded*, by Dr. W. J. Leyds.

turned upon was not the wishes of the inhabitants, or the division of the land in accordance with actual tribal occupation, but the " trade routes." The Transvaal was not to be given an inch of territory, because if she were the trade routes to the north would be in Boer and not in British hands. The Cape Premier and Lord Derby and the British Government accepted Rhodes's telegraphic policy, and the boundary was drawn so as to include the trade routes in British territory. This meant that it had to be drawn without any reference to native rights or occupation : half a tribe was left on one side and half on the other side of the line. The result was years of unrest, discontent, and fighting among the natives.

The subsequent history of British expansion in South Africa was directed almost entirely by economic motives and actually by economic organisations. In 1889 the British South Africa Company received a Royal Charter. The object of this joint-stock company, as defined in the Charter, was the acquisition and use of concessions in the country north of Bechuanaland, and the South African Republic, now known as Rhodesia. Its operations were controlled by Cecil Rhodes and his lieutenant, Dr. Jameson.

A year after the grant of the Charter the Company occupied Mashonaland with an armed force. Two years later Rhodes and Jameson raised an armed force for the invasion and occupation of Matabeleland. The terms of enlistment were significant : every trooper was to be entitled to choose for himself about nine square miles of the Matabeles' land, and to share the loot (*i.e.*, the Matabeles' only property, cattle) with the Chartered Company. The company then picked a quarrel with Lo Bengula, the Matabele king, and its mercenaries invaded his country and defeated him. By this conquest a joint-stock company, situated in 2, London Wall Buildings, London, E.C.2, claimed to become the absolute owner of 148,000 square miles of territory and 700,000 Africans situated between latitude 16 and 22 south of the equator. Here we have a good example of economic imperialism reduced to its simplest terms.

In the previous paragraphs we have been considering the nature of the imperialist expansion of European States in those cases in which they used territory already in their possession as jumping-off places for territorial aggrandisement. This process was mainly confined to the north and the south : the process by which central Africa was partitioned was somewhat different, but the economic motives behind the expansion are even more evident. If we examine the process by which Germany, Britain, and Belgium obtained a tropical African empire, we find a marked similarity of method. First semi-private or private expeditions of exploration are sent out into territory in the possession of native communities and chiefs or kings. These expeditions are always directly or indirectly associated with or controlled by commercial companies or by groups of European financiers and capitalists. Usually the explorer acts in the name of the capitalist association or joint-stock company, and in their name he proceeds to obtain or extort " treaties " from the native chiefs and rulers. These treaties are curious documents : the king or chief signs them by making a mark, and thereby proclaims to the world that he has received from the European and his company a little cloth, some bottles of gin, and the promise of protection, while he has given in exchange to the European and the company the sovereignty over the whole of his lands and people.

It is only necessary to give one or two examples in order to prove the accuracy of these statements.

The British claim to Nigeria is based ultimately upon a large number of " treaties " of this kind obtained from African emirs and rulers by agents and officers of the National African Company which subsequently became the Royal Niger Company. According to these treaties which were made between 1884 and 1892, the native rulers assert that " we cede the whole of our country (or territory) to the National African Company (Limited)." The British possession of British East Africa and Uganda is founded on similar treaties obtained by the British East Africa Company through their officers and agents from the Sultan of Zanzibar, the King of Uganda, and various native chiefs. The claim of Germany to German East Africa was based upon a large number of similar treaties obtained in 1884 by the explorer Dr. Peters, in the name of the Gesellschaft für deutsche Kolonisation which subsequently became the German East Africa Company. Lastly, the claim of King Leopold and the Belgians to the million square miles of the Belgian Congo was based on " treaties made with 450 independent African chiefs " by Stanley, in the name of an Association founded and controlled by King Leopold.

These immense acquisitions of African territory by the European States were thus directly controlled by financial capitalist groups, associations, or companies. But that was not all. These groups and companies were in close connection with and under the protection of their Governments. Thus the German East Africa Company received a Charter from the German Government in 1885 ; the British Government granted a Royal Charter to the British East Africa Company in 1885, to the Royal Niger Company in 1886, and to the British South Africa Company in 1889 ; Leopold, King of the Belgians, was the absolute controller of the association which acquired the Belgian Congo. The European Governments not only gave official support and recognition to these financial groups and joint-stock companies, which acquired sovereignty by the most dubious methods over hundreds of thousands of square miles of African territories, they allowed and encouraged them to make good their occupation of those territories by every means, including warfare against the inhabitants. And long before the occupation was effective, they handed over to these companies the administration of the countries. In the 'eighties and 'nineties of last century we have, therefore, this extraordinary phenomenon. German, British, French, and Belgian joint-stock companies or financial associations, of which the main object was the earning of profits and dividend upon capital, supported and officially recognised by their Governments, had acquired sovereignty over some two million square miles of territory, and at least fifty millions of people in Africa, and there they were allowed to remain and to reconcile the duties of government and administration with the duty of making profits.

The preceding pages will have shown that the ultimate causes and motives which produced the partition of Africa were economic. The impulse to the acquisition of these empires came from financiers and traders ; the actual acquisition was largely the work of agents and officers of joint-stock companies ; and the power of the European State was directly or indirectly placed at the service of these companies and financiers because Europeans had come to believe that the power of the European State should be used in Africa and elsewhere to promote the economic interests of its European subjects.

So far we have been considering only the causes and motives of the acquisition of empire in Africa.

We now have to examine the methods and principles upon which the European States have administered their African possessions, in order to estimate the results of the partition of Africa both upon the European and the African subjects of those States. I propose to examine first the effects of economic imperialism upon the European State and its European subjects, and then to consider its effects upon the native of Africa.

There is no doubt that those Germans, Frenchmen, and Britons who originally set out to win colonies in Africa for their countries had a very hazy notion of the nature of the African continent. Their writings and speeches show that they conceived of an African " colony " as a source of wealth to the " mother-country," because it furnished a new market for European manufactures, a source of raw materials for European industries, and a place where European capital could be lucratively invested. But they also had the old-fashioned idea that a " colony " was colonisable, that it would form a new home overseas for large numbers of emigrants from the mother country. It very soon became clear that Africa would never be colonised in the way in which America, and even Australia and New

Zealand, had been colonised. The European found that he could make his home and rear a family and do manual labour in but a very few portions of the African continent, and, even where this is possible in the north and south, the number of immigrants from the mother country into the new possession has been comparatively insignificant. In 1911 Algeria, a " white man's country," had been in the possession of France for eighty years and immense efforts had been made by the French to colonise it, yet out of a total population of five and a half million, only three-quarters of a million were Europeans, and less than 500,000 of these were Frenchmen. The population of the South African Union is now nearly six million, but only one and a quarter million are Europeans, and a large number of these are of Dutch extraction.

Algeria and South Africa have been in the hands of European States for a century or more ; they are pre-eminently " white men's countries " ; yet in both places Europeans still form only a small minority of the population. The complete failure of Europeans to colonise Africa is shown still more plainly in the case of the tropical African possessions of European States. In 1914, the four African colonies of Germany had an area of 930,000 square miles and a population of nearly twelve million ; the total white population was only 20,000. If we take the four British possessions of British East Africa, Nyasaland, Nigeria, and the Gold Coast, we find that the area is roughly 700,000 square miles, and the total population about twenty-two million ; the European population is 11,000.

African possessions have, therefore, not materially contributed to the strength of European States by providing them with colonisable territory. To what extent can they be said to have been a source of wealth to the mother country ? This question can only be answered by a reference to statistics. Only import and export figures will show the extent to which these territories have provided markets and raw materials for the industries of the mother country. As soon as these figures are examined, it will be seen that the ideas of imperialists with regard to the importance of African colonial possessions as sources of wealth are delusions.

Let us first examine the possibilities and actualities of the British tropical African possessions, Somaliland, British East Africa, Uganda, Nyasaland, Gambia, the Gold Coast, Sierra Leone, and

Nigeria. The total imports of all these possessions in the year before the war amounted in value to under £19,000,000, the total exports to under £18,000,000. The total imports of all these possessions from the United Kingdom amounted to under £9,000,000, and the total exports to the United Kingdom were under £8,000,000. On the other hand the total exports of the United Kingdom to all countries amounted to £634,000,000, and the total imports from all countries amounted to £768,000,000. Consider what these figures mean. They mean that if the United Kingdom were able to reserve the whole of its tropical African possessions as a market for its manufactures, and as a source of raw materials for its industries, the whole of these possessions would only have provided a market for two per cent. of British exports, and would have furnished only two per cent. of British imports. But no country, of course, has ever succeeded in such a monopolistic exploitation of its possessions, and in actual fact these British African possessions furnished a market for only one per cent. of British exports and provided less than one per cent. of British imports. Their economic importance to British trade and industry was about the same as that of Chile ; as a market for

British manufactures the Argentine Republic was nearly three times more important and as a source of British imports was six times more important. Could anything show more clearly the economic fallacies of imperialism ? This vast tropical African empire of Britain, acquired at great cost both in men and money, is of far less economic importance to us than the independent South American Republic of the Argentine. There is no reason to suppose that, if it were not part of the British Empire, it would cease to supply a market for our exports or to furnish us with raw materials, but, even if it did, the effect upon British trade and industry would be negligible.

The protectionist will probably argue that this startling result is due to Free Trade, and that under a system of protectionism imperial possessions can be made of great economic importance to the mother country. The experience of France, however, which is the only State to attempt to combine protectionism and imperialism on a large scale, proves that this is another imperialist delusion. The importance of the French tropical African empire to French industry is just as negligible as that of the British to British industry. The tropical African possessions of France provide a market for between one per cent. and two per cent. of French exports, and they supply between one per cent. and two per cent. of French imports. This small economic value of African possessions is not really surprising. In the first place no highly industrialised State of Europe can find an important market for its manufactured goods, except where there is an effective demand for them. In Africa under existing conditions, there cannot be such a demand. In many parts of the continent there is a very large native population, and imperialists have deluded themselves into thinking that these millions of natives can be converted into consumers of European manufactured goods. They forget the social and economic conditions under which the natives live. For instance the amount of British products which British industry can sell to the six million inhabitants of British East Africa and Uganda is limited by the amount that those six million natives can, under existing economic conditions, pay for imported products. The rate of wages paid to native labour is a good index of the purchasing power of the native population. In British East Africa the average rate of wages before the war was 2d. or 3d. a day. The money value of the total income of this native population, among which such a rate of wages rules, can scarcely exceed £5,000,000* and is probably considerably less. Out of this income the natives have first to supply themselves with food and pay taxes, and the money value of these two deductions must be at least £2,500,000. The balance is available for the purchase of European commodities. As soon as these facts are realised, it is no longer surprising to find that in 1913 the six million inhabitants of British East Africa and Uganda purchased from the United Kingdom only £1,000,000 worth of manufactured goods. The few score inhabitants of Park Lane have a far higher purchasing power and are a far better market for British industries than the millions of Africans in these British possessions.

French, German, and British imperialists are also continually speaking of tropical African possessions as rich sources of the raw materials of industry. This too is largely a delusion. The value of the raw materials produced by these territories is relatively small. Take the case of palm oil, one of the most important products of

* I include in this, of course, the value of products grown by the natives as well as money income from wages. I am told by one who knows East Africa well that the above is " a ludicrously high figure."

West Africa. The total value of all unrefined palm oil imported into the United Kingdom during 1913 was only £2,000,000, and the value of unrefined palm oil actually retained for the use of British industry was only just over £1,000,000. Compare this with the £70,000,000 worth of raw cotton, the £34,000,000 worth of wool, the £7,000,000, worth of unwrought copper, or the £6,000,000 worth of iron ore imported from other parts of the world during the same period. These figures at once explain why our African possessions play so small a part in supplying the raw materials for our industries. The products of these countries are, no doubt, valuable and industrially important, but they cannot in these respects compare with the products of the great metal producing or cotton and wool producing countries.

Nowhere is the economic fallacy of imperialism more obvious than in the doctrines of imperialists with regard to the importance of imperial possessions as sources of the raw materials of industry. The truth is that such possessions have no importance at all as special sources of supply, the reason being that no European State has hitherto succeeded in reserving the raw materials of its possessions for its own industries. The metals and agricultural products of these countries are exploited by European capitalists and joint-stock companies, which do not sell their goods to a man because he is or is not an Englishman, or because he is or is not a Frenchman, but solely because he will pay a certain price for palm oil or tin or rubber. A glance at any table of imports will prove this. Nigeria is one of the few British tropical African possessions which produces metals : it possesses tin mines for instance. According to the doctrines of imperialism Nigeria, because it is a British possession, has a peculiar value to British industry in supplying it with tin. But, if we turn to the tables of imports, we find that the United Kingdom imports only £400,000 worth of tin from Nigeria while it imports £2,000,000 worth of tin from Bolivia and nearly £1,000,000 worth of iron ore from Algeria and Tunis. If Nigeria is valuable because it is a source of tin for British industry and is within the British Empire, one might as reasonably argue that Bolivia is four times more valuable as a source of tin because it is not within the British Empire, and Algeria and Tunis are twice as valuable as sources of iron because they are within the French Empire.

The only people to whom tropical possessions are a source of considerable wealth are to be found not in the industrial classes, but in the small class of concessionaires and capitalists who actually exploit the land and labour of the tropics. On the other hand to European States themselves African and Asiatic empires have been a source, not of profit, but of expense. The budget of no European State has ever shown any credit balance from the administration of its African possessions : French and German budgets always showed considerable deficits, and although this has not been the case with the British budget, it still remains true that, if the cost of military expeditions and wars be included, the British taxpayer has paid heavily for the privilege of ruling thirty-five million Africans.

There is only one other important point with regard to the effects of economic imperialism in Africa upon Europe and Europeans, and it can be dismissed shortly. It is now widely admitted that the partition of Africa and the struggle among the Great Powers for the control of African territory had a most disastrous effect upon European international relations during the period 1880 to 1914. But few people realise how persistently the policy of imperialism in Africa urged European States into a policy of hostility to one another. For twenty-five years it was the sole important cause of the alienation of France from Britain. Egypt, and the struggle for the Nile Valley and the Niger, were the only reasons for that embittered hostility between the two nations which twice at least brought them to the very verge of war. During the same time a similar struggle for control first of Tunis, then of Tripoli, and finally of Abyssinia, embittered the relations between two States, France and Italy, which naturally should have been friendly, and was a determining factor in throwing Italy into an alliance with Germany and Austria directed against France. Lastly, African imperialism had a very large share in producing the international situation which ended in the European war. Germany's demand for " a place in the sun " was only a phrase which covered the complaint of her imperialists that they had not got their due share in the partition of Africa and the scramble for empire. The demand could not be satisfied without disturbing the *status quo* in the division of imperial spoils. This was the one really dangerous element in the animosity which steadily grew up between Germany and Britain and between Germany and France. It issued in an open struggle during the Moroccan dispute for African territory, and that dispute was only a prelude to the war.

If Britons, Frenchmen, and Germans were, what they falsely think themselves to be, rational, they would see that the economic imperialism of their States in Africa has brought upon them great evils and little good. The evils were years of international unrest and hostility, threats of war, and at last war. And the goods ? We could pride ourselves upon being an imperial people because with the help of modern rifles and machine-guns we were able to conquer and rule African savages ; a few hundred of our fellow countrymen found occupation in the administration of our conquests ; and lastly, a small number of capitalists and concessionaires made (or lost) money by exploiting the land and inhabitants of those possessions.

It remains to consider the effect of imperialism upon Africa and the Africans. The imperialist claims that the partition of Africa among European States gave to the natives law, order, and the blessings of Christianity and civilisation. It is true that European rule has usually brought with it a kind of law and order which had not previously existed in Africa. But this regular administration has in almost every case only been established after persistent and ruthless slaughter of the inhabitants in wars and through "punitive expeditions." It is too a strange use of langauge to call by the name "law and order" the savage and atrocious system of administration which was applied in the Belgian Congo, the French Congo, and German South-West Africa, and which led to the extermination of large numbers of the inhabitants. It becomes still more difficult for Europeans to make good this claim when they remember the anarchy and misery which they inflicted on Africa by deliberately extending the European war to that continent.

It is untrue that Europeans have extended the blessings of their Christianity and civilisation to Africans. There are nine million persons in Africa who are nominally Christians out of a total estimated population of 170 millions. So much for Christianity. The only way in which Europeans could have helped Africans to share in the blessings of their civilisation would have been through education. But no real attempt has been made by any European State to educate its native subjects. In Nigeria in 1917 for a population of 16,500,000, there were sixty-one Government schools, eighty-six assisted schools, and about 1,000 unassisted private schools. The Government spent on education £46,000 out of a total revenue of £3,492,000. In Uganda, where the natives pay £180,000 in direct taxation, the Government spends practically nothing on education; in a population of 3,357,000 only 50,000 children are recorded as attending the missionary schools.

If Europeans have failed to introduce their religion and neglected to introduce the spiritual blessings of their civilisation among the natives, they have succeeded in introducing their economic system. That is not surprising for it is natural that the economic motives and objects which caused the European State to enter Africa should continue to control the administrative policy of the imperial States. The main characteristics of the European capitalist economic system are (1) private individual ownership of land and the instruments of production, (2) the division of the population into economic classes, e.g., landowners, owners of capital, landless and capitalless persons working for a money wage. Such a system is almost the antithesis of the indigenous African economic system which the European found when he first

entered Africa. As a rule the African lived in
tribes and under tribal government and the
leadership of kings and chiefs. Industry, as we
know it, and large scale agriculture did not exist.
A landless and propertyless class living on money
wages paid by land-owners or capitalists did not
exist. Frequently the land was owned commun-
ally by the tribe, and, even where this was not the
case, private ownership of land in the European
sense was not known.

It was inevitable that the opening of Africa to
the penetration of Europe should modify this
system. The problem which the European
statesmen who seized African territory between
1880 and 1890 had to face was the adaptation of the
African economic system to that of Europe. Only
in rare instances was the problem faced. The
alternatives were adaptation and destruction, and
European statesmen, under the impulse of
financiers, capitalists, and traders, chose, except in
some British possessions on the west coast, the
policy of destruction.

The whole world knows in outline the methods
by which native society and the African system
were destroyed and Europe's capitalist system
fastened upon Africa. The process was revealed

first with regard to the Belgian Congo and then with regard to certain German colonies. The land is taken from the natives and alienated to European capitalists or joint-stock companies. Either by direct or by indirect compulsion the native is then forced to work upon the European's land on the European's terms. The extraordinary cruelties and brutalities which accompanied the expropriation and exploitation of the natives of the Congo and some German possessions have obscured the real lesson of those happenings. It was not the atrocities which made the system bad but the system which caused the atrocities, and the system was not confined to King Leopold's and Germany's possessions ; it is almost universal in Africa. In every tropical African possession the expropriation, exploitation, and virtual enslavement of the native inhabitants have been demanded by the white settlers and capitalists, and everywhere, except in British West Africa, this is being accomplished. A few instances will prove this. At the end of the last century the whole French Congo was subjected to precisely the same system as the Belgian Congo.* The land and its inhabitants were

* For the facts, with regard to the French Congo see *The Black Man's Burden* by E. D. Morel, Chapter X.

handed over to concessionary companies for exploitation ; all the products of the land became the property of the concessionaires ; the consequence was that the only way in which the population could keep itself from starvation was to work for the concessionaires on their own terms. The natives, seeing themselves expropriated and reduced to what was in fact slavery, revolted, and the system could only be fastened on the French Congo by the same bloody and cruel methods by which it had previously been fastened on the Belgian Congo. But the French and Belgian Congos are only extreme cases of the same evil system which is being fastened on Africa in other places by other methods. Take the case of British East Africa which is a typical example of British colonial policy in African possessions other than those upon the West Coast. The British Government in East Africa has expropriated the natives from some of the best land and alienated it to white men and joint-stock companies. The natives are relegated to Reserves. Now this process of alienation to Europeans continues with the following inevitable results. The land is useless to the white man unless he can get the native to labour on it for him, for the European does not perform manual labour in

Africa. The native, so long as he has any land on which he can work for himself, will not willingly work for wages on the land from which the European has expropriated him. Hence arises a demand from the white settler upon the Government to compel the natives to labour for him. This compulsion can be of different kinds. It may be direct legal compulsion. It may be indirect, *e.g.*, the Reserves may be cut down until the natives have insufficient land to support themselves on and thus be forced to come out and work for the white man, or a tax may be levied on all natives who do not work for white men, or the tribal machinery may be used to compel the native to leave the Reserve and work for the white men. All these methods of compulsion are asked for by the white settlers in East Africa and some of them are already in operation. For instance, the native has no legal title at all in any land even in the Reserves, and cases have already occurred of land in the Reserves being taken from a tribe and sold to Europeans. In Nyasaland a differential tax is levied upon natives not working for Europeans. In British East Africa Government instructions are now issued to native chiefs which exert pressure upon the chief to supply labour to Europeans, and the chief interprets these instructions by compelling the natives through the tribal machinery to leave the Reserve and work upon the settler's farms. Thus we have in this British possession a system of expropriation which is being followed by a system of forced labour. When it is added that before the war the average rate of wages paid by the settlers was 2d. or 3d. a day, and is now possibly 7d. or 8d., the economic evil of this system may be realised.

Those who defend this system, which is essentially one of exploitation of the African for the benefit of the European, do so usually on the ground that it is economically inevitable. The argument is that an inferior civilisation must give way before a superior, and that it is both inevitable and right that the native who cannot exploit the riches of his own country should stand aside and allow the European to do so. The premises of this argument are proved by the facts to be false. It so happens that in the British possessions on the West Coast of Africa an entirely different system of administration was for many years adopted as a policy of colonial government. In Nigeria, the Gold Coast, Gambia, and Sierra Leone the British Government has treated the land as the property

of the native communities, has refused to alienate
it to Europeans, and has to some extent encouraged
the native to make the most economical use of it
under modern conditions. The result has shown
that the African, if he be given the chance, is
perfectly competent to take his place as a free man
in the world's economic system, that he is able to
make an economic use of his own land and supply
the world with the agricultural products needed by
the industries and industrial populations of Europe
and America. The following facts are sufficient
to prove this statement. In British West Africa
the native, working as a free man on his own land,
produces palm kernels, cocoa, ground nuts,
cotton, and rubber, and the total exports from these
possessions varies from 10s. to £4 or £5 per head
of the population : in British East Africa and
Nyasaland the native, unwillingly and often under
compulsion, is employed by white settlers and
joint stock companies to produce coffee, sisal,
ground nuts, cotton, rubber, oil seeds, hides and
skins, and the total exports are less than 2s. in the
one case and less than 7s. in the other per head of
the population. It is, of course, true that the
fertility and wealth of West Africa is considerably
greater than that of East Africa, but the figures at

least prove conclusively that native labour employed on native owned land is not inferior in economic efficiency to forced native labour on European owned land.

BIBLIOGRAPHY

For the whole subject of economic imperialism in Africa the reader should refer to

(1) *Empire and Commerce in Africa*, by Leonard Woolf (Allen and Unwin and Labour Research Department).

(2) Labour Party Pamphlet on Africa.

(3) *Africa : Slave or Free ?* by J. H. Harris (Student Christian Movement).

(4) *The Black Man's Burden*, by E. D. Morel (National Labour Press).

(5) *The Chartered Millions*, by J. H. Harris (Swarthmore Press).

CHAPTER III

ECONOMIC IMPERIALISM IN ASIA

THE methods by which the lands and peoples of Africa have been subjected to Europeans and delivered over to economic exploitation are the ancient methods of war, conquest, and annexation. European States have absorbed the kingdoms and countries of Africa only under the primeval right of the stronger to enslave the weaker. It is a comparatively unimportant fact that slavery in the modern world no longer generally takes the form of crude physical compulsion and legal ownership in the body of another man or woman. The modern economic form of slavery may be less distressing to the consciences of sentimental people, but it is just as effective as the old.

Economic imperialism in Asia has developed some peculiar features which distinguish it from the African variety and which deserve careful study. They are, however, far more complicated than the comparatively simple phenomena which we studied in the previous chapter, and it is therefore not possible in the space at my disposal to do anything more than indicate a few of their most important characteristics.

The history of Asia in the last half of the nineteenth century is very similar to that of Africa. We find the same violent and sudden impact and penetration of Europe and the European State, and the outburst of imperialism began at the same time, about 1880. In some parts of Asia it pursued precisely the same course as it did in Africa. The European State entered, conquered, and annexed Asiatic territory on the same pretexts and with the same declared economic objects as in the other continent. For instance in 1883 France began an attack upon the Chinese Empire by a military expedition which resulted in the French annexation of Tonking and Annam. In 1886 Britain invaded Burma, deposed its king, and annexed the country. But in the greater part of Asia the policy of direct conquest and annexation was not pursued, and in 1914 only India, large portions of Russia in Asia, French Indo-China, the Malay States, The Straits Settlements, Hong-kong, and Java had been incorporated in the empires of European States. But the rest of Asia, which includes the Ottoman

Empire, Persia, China, and Japan, was not left untouched or unmolested by Europe. Into these countries European civilisation, particularly in its economic manifestations, penetrated deeply, and, while not subjected directly to the political system of Europe, they were all, with the exception of Japan, brought under the indirect control of European States. In other words Turkey, Persia, and China were not openly partitioned or annexed, but the power of European States was brought to bear indirectly upon them, mainly with the object of promoting the economic interests of Europeans. I propose to examine briefly the methods and results of this process in China, but a word must be said first as to the reasons why the system of conquest and absorption was not applied to these Asiatic countries.

Before the war the break up of Turkey, Persia, and China was repeatedly prophesied as imminent, but it never actually took place. One reason undoubtedly which saved a nominal independence to these countries may be found in the fact that during the period of the first and most vigorous outburst of imperialism, 1880 to 1890, the Great Powers of Europe were too busy carving up Africa to allow of their giving serious attention to the much more difficult task of carving up Asia. But when there was nothing left of any great value to seize in Africa, imperialist jealousies had been thoroughly aroused and were so acute that it was clear that no overt partition of Turkey or China could take place without the very great risk of a European war. It was extremely doubtful whether the civilised proletariats of Europe could be inveigled into slaughtering one another on any large scale in order to destroy the independence of Turks, Persians, and Chinese, and economic imperialism had to make the best of other methods until providentially the peoples of Europe began to slaughter one another on the largest possible scale in order to end war, preserve the independence of small nations, and make the world safe for democracy. It is too early to speak with certainty, but it looks as if one of the results of the war has been to destroy a good deal of such independence as remained to Turkey, Persia, China, and all Asiatic peoples other than the Japanese.

The conquest and absorption of Asiatic peoples is far more difficult than that of Africans. Everywhere in Asia there are old and highly developed civilisations with complex political institutions and economic systems which may be different from, but are not necessarily inferior to, those of Europe. The resistance to conquest and absorption was therefore quite different in Asia and in Africa, and the Great Powers soon realised that they could not treat the descendants of Solyman the Magnificent, Tamerlaine, and the T'ang emperors, in the way in which they had treated King Mwanga of Uganda or the chiefs of Timbuktu. This resistance of Asia to Europe was, of course, enormously intensified towards the end of the last century by the rise to power of Japan. The westernisation of Japan was in fact itself a reaction against the penetration and economic imperialism of Europe in Asia. The Japanese deliberately adopted the political, military, and economic system of Europe in order to protect themselves against political absorption and economic exploitation. The success of this adaptation was so rapid and so complete that Japan was not only able to defy the imperialist Powers but to insist upon being admitted to their ranks. The partition of China seemed to be indefinitely postponed when the Great Powers realised that they would have to reckon with Japan who was most favourably situated for taking a hand in such a partition and was strong enough to insist upon no small share of the prey.

These are the reasons which forced economic imperialism to proceed by more indirect and delicate methods in Asia than in Africa. Nevertheless, the objects and results of these methods were not essentially dissimilar, for they consisted in the indirect use of the power of the European State in order to promote the economic interest of Europeans in Asia. I propose to indicate some of the more important characteristics of this form of economic imperialism as they appear in the history of the treatment of China by the Great Powers.

It must never be forgotten that economic imperialism is a phase in the problem of the clash of civilisations. The history of China during the last century cannot be properly understood unless this fact is borne in mind. When the nineteenth century opened there were probably between 300 and 400 million Chinese living under a Chinese Government and a social and economic system of great complexity. Their institutions, their religion, their art and literature were all deeply rooted in the most ancient of civilisations. Like most other races, they considered themselves and their civilisation to be the best in the world, and, as has always been the case in the world's history, this belief was fostered by the fact that the only civilisation which they knew was their own. The Far East had had practically no contact with Europe or America, and the only peoples whom the Chinese knew were the Japanese and the Koreans, and other races of the continent of Asia whom they had from time to time conquered. But those changes in the structure of European society which we call the industrial revolution were bound eventually to bring Europe into close touch with China. The new European economic system implied that the beliefs and desires of Europeans drove them out to find new markets and supplies of the raw materials of industry with a persistence and on a scale unknown in previous centuries. And the new industrial system gave them the means, in the ships, the railways, and the intricate and powerful organisation of commerce and finance, of imposing their economic will and their system upon any people which could not resist them politically.

The first impact of this new European economic system upon China can be observed in the first half of the nineteenth century. Gradually the question of foreign trade between China and the manufacturing nations of the West became an acute one. The Chinese, believing that their own civilisation was infinitely superior to that of other peoples, desired to have no relations whether of trade or anything else with the barbarians, but a growing swarm of British, French, American, and German traders gathered around the Chinese coasts insisting in the name of civilisation that China should open her doors to the products of western industries. Here immediately arose a clash between two civilisations, between two ideals of life and two economic systems. The merchants and traders at once appealed to their European Governments to use the power of the State in order to force the European economic system upon China. In the first part of the century economic imperialism was not accepted as a principle of policy, and no European Government admitted that it was justified or obliged to use its force directly in order to promote the economic interests of its subjects or to compel the Chinese to open its country to European trade. Nevertheless the action of the merchants and traders actually led to the use of the European State's power for these ends as early as 1842. The Chinese attempted to enforce the prohibition of the import of opium by foreign merchants though Canton. In 1839, the Chinese

Imperial Commissioner at Canton demanded the surrender of opium in the hands of some British merchants, and, when this was refused, the factories were blockaded and the British community expelled from Canton. Here was the merchants' opportunity ; British subjects had suffered insult and loss, and it was the duty of their Government to demand an apology and compensation. The British Government adopted the view of their merchants and the result was the Opium War and the Treaty of Nanking, 1842. The treaty provided that China should cede Hongkong to Britain, should open five ports to British trade, and should allow British consuls to represent Britain in the treaty ports.

The next sixteen years were occupied in a hopeless struggle of China to prevent the European economic system penetrating into the country. Palmerston was in power in England, and his policy, as the *Cambridge Modern History* puts it, was to " take advantage of the first occasion to coerce the Chinese into relations of a normal character." The opportunity occurred in 1856, and a British fleet, subsequently joined by a French squadron, applied the coercion. Canton was occupied, and the Chinese Imperial Commissioner was taken prisoner. China then signed the Treaty of Tientsin, 1858, by which she agreed to allow diplomatic representation of Britain at Peking, to grant the free right of travel in China to British subjects, to open the Yangtse river to British ships, and several new ports to British trade, and to allow the import of opium. Similar treaties were signed with France, Russia, and the United States, but the Chinese made one last desperate effort to avoid the inevitable and refused to allow the British representative to enter Peking. A naval and military expedition which captured the Taku forts and destroyed the Peking Summer Palace finally taught the Chinese the hopelessness of fighting against European civilisation, and the signing of the Treaty of Peking, 1860, completed the opening up of China to Europe.

I have given the facts in the previous paragraph in order that the reader may understand the general nature of the international problem which was growing up in the Far East. The penetration of Europe's new industrial and economic system into China was probably inevitable. Quite apart from the overwhelming force which that system placed at the disposal of European States, in an age of steamships and railways no nation can successfully practise a policy of excluding foreigners and foreign trade. But the economic penetration of China created a situation of very great complexity and difficulty. Chinese governmental and economic institutions and methods were completely unable to deal with the elaborate and powerful machinery of European industry and trade. In the clash between these two civilisations friction was inevitable, and, if it came to a question of force, China was helpless in the hands of Europe. But there were two alternative paths which Europe might have followed in the process of " opening up " China. The first was the path of economic exploitation, pure and simple ; it was open to Europeans to employ the whole elaborate economic machinery of their industry and commerce, backed by the irresistible political power of their States, to promote their own immediate economic interests in China. The other was the path of co-operation rather than of exploitation : the European and his State might have used their knowledge and power to help the Chinese to adapt their political and economic system to that of Europe and to obtain their fair share of the wealth which the European system was capable of creating.

It will be argued that the second alternative was

impossibly utopian. But it was not; it was actually tried with success in a limited field. In the middle of last century, the Chinese fiscal and customs system was in principle very similar to that of Rome in the time of Julius Cæsar. It is therefore not surprising that it proved hopelessly inadequate for dealing with European trade and traders. It was not only that the Chinese Customs Service and the European merchants became steadily more corrupt; the existence of a mediæval organisation resulted in China being unable to assert its fiscal rights against the foreign importer. By 1854 smuggling and the evasion of duties had become the rule rather than the exception, and in such circumstances it was naturally the more honest trader who was penalised. The foreign consuls were continually being called upon by their nationals to interfere, particularly in Shanghai, when breaches of the treaties or unfair treatment were alleged, and the governmental anarchy was enormously increased by the Taiping rebellion. In 1854, things had become so intolerable that a proposal was made and an agreement signed between the British, American, and French consuls on the one side and the Chinese Customs authorities at Shanghai on the other whereby foreign customs inspectors were to be appointed by the Chinese. It was distinctly stated in the agreement that these appointments were necessitated by the " impossibility of obtaining customs house officials with the necessary qualifications as to probity, vigilance, and knowledge of foreign languages, required for the enforcement of a close observance of treaty and custom-house regulations." A board of three inspectors, one American, one French, and one British, was appointed. The system proved successful in Shanghai, and four years later was extended to all the treaty ports. In 1863, Mr. Robert Hart was appointed Inspector-General of Customs by the Chinese Government, and under his long administration the whole customs service was reorganised. Two facts with regard to Sir Robert Hart's achievement deserve notice. From the first he made the service international. In 1864 it consisted of six English, two American, one French, and one German official in charge of collectorates. In 1912 the executive branch " included a total of 354, of whom 145 were English, fourteen American, thirty-two French, thirty-eight German, sixteen Russian, thirty-three Japanese, fifty of nine other nationalities, and twenty-six Chinese." This international service

rapidly developed an *esprit de corps* of its own.
From the first " the commissioners of customs
acted on the assumption that China retained all
sovereign rights which had not been specifically
granted away by the treaties, an assumption of
which no one now doubts the correctness." In
other words the European customs officials considered it their duty to build up for the Chinese
Government a service which would protect the
legitimate interests and the rights of the Chinese
people. Their efforts were met with hostility and
opposition both from the foreign traders and the
foreign consuls, but they were successful, and,
while everywhere else domestic corruption and
foreign exploitation were bringing ruin on China,
in the customs administration the Chinese were
being consistently helped to protect their own
economic interests.*

These facts show that it was quite possible for
Europe to co-operate with the Chinese in such a
way as to adapt Chinese organisation and government to the necessities of the modern economic
world. No one to-day will deny that the co-operation of East and West in the customs administration

* The facts and quotations in this paragraph are taken from
The International Relations of the Chinese Empire, Vol. II, by
H. B. Morse.

ultimately benefited both China and Europe. But the experiment was not repeated. In the last quarter of the century the policy of economic imperialism asserted itself, and everywhere Europeans ruthlessly applied their doctrine of international economic competition. China became, like Africa, merely a field for economic exploitation, a rich land where the trader could buy cheap and sell dear or the financier win high dividends. In this struggle for profits and dividends Europeans of every nationality tried to enlist the power of their own State for their own advantage.

The process began in 1884, with the declaration of the French protectorate over Annam. The act was tantamount to the staking out of a French claim to southern China, and it led directly to the formulation of the policy of " spheres of interest " by the imperialist Powers of Europe.

Jules Ferry had defended the Tonking expedition in the French Chamber on economic grounds, namely that it would open up the rich and populous provinces of China to French economic penetration. And the French soon showed that they were prepared to use the power of their State for economic purposes in China. By the treaty forced upon China in 1885, and two treaties subsequently signed in 1887, France obtained what seemed to be a privileged economic position in southern China. A differential duty in favour of France was to be levied on all goods passing between Tonking and the Chinese provinces of Yunnan and Kwangsi, and it was provided that, if in this region China should build railways, France would give " every facility to procure in France the personnel she might need."

This was the beginning of the use of the European State's power indirectly to secure economic advantages for its citizens in China. As the century waned, more and more pressure was exerted in the same direction by the imperialist Powers upon China, and a violent struggle between those Powers for economic advantages ensued. The exactions of France in 1885 and the next decade were continually countered by Britain who demanded and obtained similar territorial and economic advantages. Thus in 1886 China was compelled to recognise British sovereignty over Burma, and in 1890 over Sikkim. But for the reasons stated above, the political break up of China which seemed not improbable in 1885 was postponed, and the real attack of European imperialism upon the Chinese did not develop fully until the last five years of the century. It was then that the policy of spheres of interest was elaborated. The year 1897 marks the culmination of this policy. Russia seized Port Arthur and the Liaotung peninsula, Germany Kiaochau, Britain Wei-hai-wei, and France Kuangchouwan. These disguised annexations were not made merely for their own sake, they were intended to be used and were used for the purpose of exacting economic privileges from the Chinese Government. Each imperialist Power earmarked for its nationals certain parts of the Chinese Empire, e.g., France, the southern provinces, and Britain the Yangtsze Valley, which were to be reserved for economic exploitation. This exploitation mainly took the form of concessions for the building of railways or the working of mines to French, British, German, Russian financiers in the various spheres of interest.

The main point to notice is that this economic exploitation was ruthlessly carried out, without regard for the interests of the Chinese and in the interests of groups of foreign financiers supported by their Governments. One example is sufficient to show the way in which the power of the European State was used in China for the purposes of econo-

mic exploitation. In 1897 a Belgian syndicate
obtained a concession for building a railway from
Peking to Hankow. The British, not without
reason, suspected that behind the Belgian syndicate
were French and Russians, and Lord Salisbury
informed the British representative in China that
" a concession of this nature is no longer a commercial or industrial enterprise, and becomes a
political movement against the British interests in
the region of the Yangtsze. You should inform
the Tsungli-Yamen (*i.e.*, the Chinese Government)
that her Majesty's Government cannot possibly
continue to co-operate in a friendly manner in
matters of interest to China, if, while preferential
advantages are conceded to Russia in Manchuria
and to Germany in Shantung, these or other
foreign powers should also be offered special
openings or privileges in the region of the
Yangtsze. Satisfactory proposals will be forth-
coming if the Chinese Government will invite the
employment of British capital in the development
of those provinces." When the Chinese persisted
in granting the Belgian concession, the British
Minister presented an ultimatum to the Chinese
Government. He informed that Government that
" Her Majesty's Government considered that they

had been badly treated by China in the matter of railway concessions, and now demanded from the Chinese Government the right for British merchants to build the following lines upon the same terms as those granted in the case of the Belgian line : Tientsin to Chinkiang (to be shared, if desired, with the Germans and Americans), Honan and Shansi, Peking syndicate lines to the Yangtsze ; Kowloon to Canton ; Pukou to Sinyang ; Soochow to Hangchow, with extension to Ningpo." The British Minister was directed by his Government to inform the Chinese Government that " unless they agree at once, we shall regard their breach of faith concerning the Peking-Hangkow Railway as an act of deliberate hostility against this country, and shall act accordingly. After consultation with the Admiral, you may give them the number of days or hours you think proper within which to send their reply." The Chinese Government, " being aware of the concentration of the fleet," writes an American historian, " conceded everything. Thus did Great Britain obtain her railway concessions. The total length of the lines conceded amounted to 2,800 miles extending over ten provinces, as compared to 1,530 Russian miles, the rest of the nations falling way below the Russian figure.   To England

fell the lion's share of the ' battle of concessions,'
as Lord Salisbury properly styled this ' peaceful '
conflict."*

The other imperialist Powers and their financiers,
although they may not have obtained as big a share
of the loot in this battle as Britain did, adopted no
less brutal and ruthless measures of exaction. It
is impossible here to unravel the complicated
history of this international competition for the
exploitation of China. What is more important
for our purpose is to take a rapid survey of the
results. For several years the battle of concessions
raged with increasing violence between the groups
of financiers, supported by their Governments.
This struggle proved ruinous to China. In the
first place no attempt was made to safeguard the
interests of the Chinese. China's communications, and much of her mineral wealth was mortgaged to foreign financiers, whose sole object was
the making of profits. The railways or the concessions were in the hands of different groups of
bitter competitors. In the competition for the
right of exploitation loans were made for railway
construction with little or no safeguards for

* The facts and quotations in this paragraph come from
Foreign Financial Control in China, by T. W. Overlach (Macmillan Co., New York).

adequate control over the expenditure, and the corruption of Chinese officials hastened the ruin of the country. Every possible source of Chinese revenue was mortgaged to secure the interest on these foreign loans. The Chinese themselves saw with growing anger and dismay the exploitation by foreign financiers, corrupting their Government and draining the wealth of their country. They saw that this policy of exploitation was openly supported by the bayonets and fleets of the imperialist Powers. The first result was an outburst of hostility, in the Boxer rebellion, against all foreigners. The events of 1900 are well known. The outbreak against foreigners, which resulted in the siege of the Legations in Peking, was put down by a military expedition of the Great Powers against the Chinese capital. The Christian Powers of the West, who had directly provoked this outbreak by robbing China of territory and by forcing her to mortage the wealth of her people to their financiers, then proceeded to exact from her an indemnity of £67,000,000,* presumably as a fine upon an Asiatic people for resisting the aggression and economic imperialism of Europe.

* Note that this indemnity is over one-third of the indemnity imposed by Germany on France in 1871.

The seizure of Chinese territory by France,
Germany, Russia and Britain in 1897, the con-
tinual use by these States of the threat of force in
order to extort economic concessions, the cynical
exaction of the huge indemnity in 1901, had not
escaped the attention of Japan. Japanese statesmen unanimously were of opinion that European
imperialism had only begun its task of exploiting
and robbing China, and that, if Japan was not to be
left out in the cold, she would have immediately to
assert her claim to a share in the victim. At the
moment the imperialist Power most dangerous to
Japanese interests in the Far East appeared to be
Russia who by the seizure of Port Arthur and the
Liaotung peninsula in 1897, and her penetration
and exploitation of Manchuria, had approached
very near the door of Japan and already threatened
to cut her off from the nearest markets on the
mainland. The aggressive imperialism of Europe
helped to throw the whole power in Japan into the
hands of militarist imperialists and these states-
men-soldiers laid their plans well. Having pro-
tected their flank by the alliance with Britain, they
suddenly called a halt to the Russian designs, and,
when their demands were refused, they fought and
beat the Russian Empire. By the Treaty of

Portsmouth, 1905, which ended the war, Japan became the heir to Russia's economic rights in Manchuria and ever since that date she has shown herself an apt pupil of European imperialism. By political pressure and economic exploitation she now holds a dominating position in China and the Far East.

Meanwhile the economic ruin of China proceeded. It is true that after 1905 the competition between the imperialist States and their groups of financiers was modified. The Russo-Japanese war and other events had shown clearly that this competition to exploit China, if carried to its logical conclusion, not only led to expensive wars between the competitors but reduced the financial profits which might be squeezed out of the Chinese people. International competition now gave way to a curious form of international co-operation. The chief financial interests of Britain, France, Russia, Germany, Japan, and subsequently America, joined together in a *consortium*. Under this system the several financial groups were still backed by their Governments, but elaborate arrangements were made for sharing the loans made to and the economic concessions granted by China. This, however, did not mean that any real attempt was made to safeguard Chinese rights or interests, for the object of the *consortium* was the financial interests of the *consortium*. The anti-foreign feeling among the Chinese continued, and, having failed in their attempt to deal with the foreigner directly by force, they next turned their attention to their own Government upon whom, not without reason, they laid a good deal of the blame for their exploitation. The movement towards political democracy began immediately after the death of the old Dowager Empress Tseushi in 1908, and a National Assembly was elected and met in 1910. But the annexation of Korea by Japan in the same year enfuriated the Chinese and their anger was visited on their own Government.

The result was the Revolution of 1911.

But economic imperialism sets no store by republics. The economic ruin of China which began under the monarchy has been completed under the republic. Instead of helping the new republic to get upon its feet, Europe and Japan have continued the system of economic exploitation. Civil war has been fomented and fostered by foreign loans to corrupt generals and politicians who have squandered them on their armies or have taken the simpler and more direct course of putting them straight into their own pockets. Japan, whom the war temporarily relieved of all rivals in the Far East, seized the opportunity of increasing enormously both her political and economic hold over China. She is now established in Germany's place in Shantung and in Russia's in Manchuria ; she has a large army in Siberia ; her banks and financiers have made enormous loans to the Chinese militarists, loans which place those militarists in her power ; in 1915 she presented an ultimatum, and " Twenty-one Demands " to China which resulted in her obtaining large economic concessions. This situation has created a violent feeling among the Chinese against Japan and has already given rise to an effective boycott of Japanese goods. Meanwhile, however, economic imperialism has completed its task : civil war in China is endemic ; the Government is hopelessly corrupt ; the finances are in chaos ; large portions of Chinese territory are occupied by foreign armies ; the revenue is all mortgaged to pay the interest on foreign loans from which the Chinese have derived little or no benefit and infinite loss ; and by a system of mingled fraud and force foreigners now hold in their hands China's communications and a large part of her mineral wealth.

BIBLIOGRAPHY

For the history of China, and the effect of economic imperialism there, the reader should refer to

(1) *International Relations of the Chinese Empire*, by H. B. Morse.

(2) *Anglo-Chinese Commerce and Diplomacy*, by A. J. Sargent.

(3) *Foreign Financial Control in China*, by T. W. Overlach (Macmillan, New York).

(4) *Foreign Rights and Interests in China*, by W. W. Willoughby (John Hopkins Press, U.S.A.).

For the history of Japan and her Far Eastern Policy, the reader may refer to

(1) *The Development of Japan*, by K. S. Latourette (Macmillan, New York).

(2) *Japan at the Cross Roads*, by A. M. Pooley (Allen & Unwin).

(3) *The Far East Unveiled*, by Frederic Coleman (Cassell).

(4) *The Mastery of the Far East*, by A. J. Brown (Bell & Sons).

(5) *Democracy and the Eastern Question*, by T. F. Millard (Allen & Unwin).

CHAPTER IV

CAUSES AND RESULTS

THE two previous chapters have shown us a policy, which I have called economic imperialism, at work in Asia and Africa. Its manifestations are, as I said at the beginning, only part of that world movement which has led to the penetration of Asia and Africa by the political and economic system of Europe. We have here an international problem which centres round the relations between western civilisation and the civilisations of Africa and the East. I have endeavoured to prove, within the limits of the space at my disposal, my original statement that the active principle in a civilisation or in a policy is men's beliefs and desires. The treatment of Africans and Chinese by Europeans and their States has been primarily determined by the political and economic beliefs and motives with which Europeans have approached Africa and China.

If we turn back and examine the general results of the events and policies analysed in the two previous chapters, we are forced to the conclusion that European policy has led to the subjection and economic exploitation of the African and to subjection or anarchy and economic exploitation in China. The result cannot be surprising to anyone who has studied the beliefs and desires which underlie western civilisation. We live in an era which has been correctly called the age of capitalism. It is an age of capitalism because the whole structure of our society is based upon certain economic motives. Society in Europe is now founded upon economic competition, and the dominating influence in that competition is capital and the holders of capital. The making of profits, buying cheap and selling dear, these are the principles of a capitalistic society, and the economic motives which result from accepting these principles determine the actions not only of the holders of capital but of every class in the community, from the capitalist to the artist or worker.

Economic imperialism is only the logical application of capitalism and its principles to internationalism. Europeans have, as we have seen, approached Africa and Asia from the point of view : " What profit, what economic advantage can we get out of these two continents ? " The answer is obvious to anyone who has been educated in the school of capitalism ; just as the holder of capital in Europe has been enabled to exploit the worker and consumer economically for his own profit, so the white man, armed with the power of the modern State, and the weapons of modern war, and the technical knowledge and machinery of modern industry and modern finance, can reduce to subjection, and then exploit economically for his own profit, the land and labour of the less developed Asiatic and African. Hence, just as in national society in Europe there have appeared in the last century clearly defined classes, capitalists and workers, exploiters and exploited, so too in international society there have appeared clearly defined classes, the imperialist Powers of the West and the subject races of Africa and the East, the one ruling and exploiting, the other ruled and exploited.

The results of the policy of economic imperialism pursued by this country and the other imperialist powers can hardly be viewed with satisfaction or equanimity. Political subjection, exploitation, and economic slavery are never pleasant to their victims. Sixty years experience of the blessings of

European rule and civilisation have resulted in Europeans being hated by their subjects from Timbuktu to Peking. And we are only at the beginning of the reaction against the cupidity and violence of western nations. India and Egypt have already brought it home to us in this country that neither the Asiatic nor the African will submit indefinitely to the despotic government and exploitation of a European State, and that the time comes when that rule can only be maintained by " controlled rifle fire," machine guns, and bombing aeroplanes. France and Britain have been engaged since the end of the war in extending their system of economic exploitation over vast areas of Africa and the Middle East. We must face the fact that every year the hostility of "subject races" to the subjection of Western Powers will increase, and the great capitalistic Empires of Britain and France will more and more have to be defended by force against Western rivals and imposed by force upon their Asiatic and African subjects.

Those who defend imperialism and capitalism will argue that there is no practical alternative to this system. This view is only correct if it be inevitable for men to continue to hold the false beliefs and to be moved by the disastrous motives which underly imperialism. For there is another and a diametrically opposite system open to the Powers and peoples of Europe which, as a matter of fact, they have pledged themselves to adopt in the most formal and solemn manner. At the end of the war there was incorporated in the peace treaties, signed by nearly all the States of the world, the Covenant of the League of Nations. Article 22 of the Covenant deals with the Asiatic territory of the Ottoman Empire and the African possessions of Germany. It pledges the Western Powers to institute in those territories a system which is the antithesis of imperialism, the mandatory system. The principle of the mandatory system is defined by the article as follows : that the " well-being and development of " the peoples of these African and Asiatic territories, " form a sacred trust of civilisation," that " the tutelage of such peoples should be entrusted to advanced nations, . . . and that this tutelage should be exercised by them as Mandatories on behalf of the League," and that " securities for the performance of this trust should be embodied in this Covenant."

Since the signing of the Covenant it has become clear that there is no intention on the part of the statesmen of the Great Powers honestly to carry out either the spirit or letter of this article. The League, as it exists to-day, and its Mandate system are both shams, and Article 22 is simply being used to obscure the fact that France and Britain are obtaining large accessions of territory for economic exploitation in Africa and Asia. This is not surprising. The States which are members of the League are capitalist States, organised on a basis of capitalistic imperialism ; the statesmen who signed the Covenant are capitalist imperialists ; the peoples in whose name they signed accept the beliefs and desires of capitalism as the principles of their private lives and of their public policies. So long as Western States are organised on these principles and men accept these beliefs and desires of capitalism and imperialism, they will not, in fact, regard the land and peoples of Asia and Africa as " a sacred trust of civilisation " but as a field for grabbing a profit from the oil of Mosul or for obtaining cheap land and cheaper labour.

But it is not true that human beings never change their beliefs and desires, and, if they did so with regard to capitalism and economic imperialism, the mandatory system might well open a new era in the relations between Asia and Africa and western civilisation. I propose to examine shortly in these last pages the way in which the mandatory system might be applied in the two cases which we have investigated in the previous chapters, namely, Africa and China.

Article 22 lays it down that the peoples of Africa and certain peoples of Asia are " not yet able to stand by themselves under the strenuous conditions of the modern world." We have seen that there is a good deal to be said for this opinion. Africans and even a highly civilised people like the Chinese are not able at once to adapt themselves to the world's changed conditions which have resulted from industrial and other developments in Europe. Intercourse between them and Europe is inevitable, and, in order to adapt themselves to the new conditions, they would require considerable assistance from Europeans. Moreover, fifty years of capitalistic imperialism have left the African in the depths of ignorance, poverty, and economic slavery, and have reduced China to anarchy and economic chaos. The European must himself help in undoing the evil which he has caused if it is to be undone rapidly.

The Covenant proposes therefore, that the " well-being and development of these peoples " shall be publicly recognised as a " sacred trust of civilisation," and that that trust shall be assumed by all nations united in the League. The League must perform its trust by helping these peoples to adapt themselves to the strenuous conditions of the modern world. The Covenant, again rightly recognises that the problem is not the same for all peoples. Some, like the Chinese, and probably all Asiatics, are capable of governing themselves as independent nations, provided that they can look to Europeans for honest administrative or expert advice and assistance, and for the means necessary to the economic development of their countries. Others, *e.g.*, the Africans, are probably not in a position immediately to take over the entire administration of their countries, and will require at first to be governed by a mandatory, whose main purpose should be to promote their material well-being and educate them to govern themselves.

How could this general system be applied to China and Africa ? The Covenant which was adopted by capitalist imperialist statesmen, who desired to cloak a policy of capitalist imperialistic annexations, proposes that the League shall in each case entrust the mandated areas to a particular State as its mandatory. The object of this proposal is plain. Britain is to be called a mandatory in German East Africa and Mesopotamia, and France a mandatory in Cameroon and Syria; and the world will go on as before, except that in practice German East Africa and Mesopotamia will be part of the British, and Cameroon and Syria part of the French empire. But if the mandatory system were honestly applied in the more advanced countries of Asia, like China and Syria, there would be no need to give a mandate over them to any particular State. China, as we have seen, would be perfectly able to manage her own affairs provided that she could look to Europeans for advice and assistance. She would require the assistance of experts and administrators in order to adapt her governmental system to modern conditions. The kind of assistance required by her is that which was actually given to her in the international Customs Service. She needs it to-day particularly for the re-organisation of her finances, the whole of her transport system, the development of her mineral wealth, and for education. Moreover, she will also probably have to look to Europe and America for a considerable amount of capital which will be required for the development of her economic resources. Now all this assistance could be given, provided that the League itself honestly accepted the " mandate for China " and made the " well-being and development " of the Chinese a " sacred trust " of the League and civilisation.   If the League were an honest League and were not dominated by Powers whose whole object is the economic exploitation of the Chinese and the riches of China, it could take the following steps to-morrow :

(1) It would return all the territory taken from the Chinese during the last fifty years.

(2) It would carry out honestly the principle of the Open Door in China.

(3) It would return to the Chinese all the rail-ways and economic concessions extorted from them.

(4) It would forbid the financing of civil war by foreign Powers.

(5) It would help the Chinese to put their finances in order.   This would probably require an international loan to China and some powers of financial supervision and control for the League.

(6) It would supply the Chinese with European experts and advisers for the re-organisation of the Chinese railway system, the opening up of mines, education, etc.

The application of the professed principles of

the Covenant to Africa would be somewhat different. Here it would be necessary at first to have a mandatory responsible for the government of the country. Many people believe that the League could not itself undertake the actual administration of territory and that in such cases it would be necessary for it to delegate its trust to a particular State. There is no real reason why the League should not be able to administer territory through an international commission, but the system would also work with a particular State as the League's mandatory, provided that the League clearly laid down the principles on which the administration should be carried on and retained the power to see that the mandatory strictly carried out the terms of the mandate. In either case, if the League really made " the well-being and development of " the African the sole principle of government, it would have to take the following steps in Africa :

(1) It would declare the land to be the property of the native communities, and it would prohibit the alienation of the land to Europeans. It would see that every native family had a sufficient amount of land for its support. Where this was impossible owing to the previous alienation of land to

Europeans, it would, by cancelling or re-purchasing concessions, re-enter on sufficient alienated land. It would encourage the native population to make the most economic use of its land by every possible means, and particularly by providing agricultural education, expert instructors, model farms, etc.

(2) It would prohibit absolutely every kind of compulsory or forced labour, and any kind of influence or pressure upon natives to work for Europeans.

(3) It would make it its primary duty to educate the African with a view both to his economic and political freedom. Its object would be to give the native the knowledge without which he cannot take his place as a free man in the " strenuous conditions of the modern world." That implies that sufficient primary schools should be provided to enable every African child to obtain primary education, and that higher education and technical education be provided with a view to educating natives to become doctors, agricultural experts, etc., and to fill the administrative posts in the government of their country.

(4) It would immediately give the native local self-government, and gradually develop a full system of responsible government.